Vula Bevalile

LETTERS FROM A YOUNG DOCTOR

Maithri
Goonetilleke

Vula Bevalile

LETTERS FROM A YOUNG DOCTOR

Maithri
Goonetilleke

With a foreword by Wayne Dyer

ILURA PRESS

ILURA PRESS
PO Box 680
Elsternwick Victoria 3185 Australia
www.ilurapress.com

Copyright © Maithri Goonetilleke 2014

Published in Australia in 2014

First edition published in Australia in 2013

All rights reserved.
Without limiting the rights under copyright above, no part of
this book may be reproduced, stored in a retrieval system, or
transmitted in any form or by any means electronic, mechanical,
photocopying, or otherwise without the prior permission of both
the copyright owner and the publisher of this book.

Goonetilleke, Maithri (author).
Vula Bevalile: Letters from a Young Doctor / Maithri Goonetilleke;
With a Foreword by Wayne Dyer.
2nd edition.
9781921325267 (hardback)

Cover design and typesetting:
Ilura Design – www.iluradesign.com

Cover images:
'Kids in a Cave' © Ferdinandreus – dreamstime.com
'Old Fabric' © Sirikul2010 – dreamstime.com
'Maithri with Busiswa Ndzinisa' © John Couch 2011

Printed and bound by Tingleman Media Group, Springvale, Victoria.

'Things aren't all so tangible and sayable as people would usually have us believe; most experiences are unsayable, they happen in a space that no word has ever entered.'

– Rainer Maria Rilke, *Letters to a Young Poet*

*

TO THE PEOPLE OF SWAZILAND

I offer all due respect and gratitude to the ruler and leaders of the Kingdom of Swaziland for allowing us to continue to serve the Swazi people.

*

While the stories in this collection are true and accurate, in many instances the names of patients and clients have been changed to protect confidentiality.

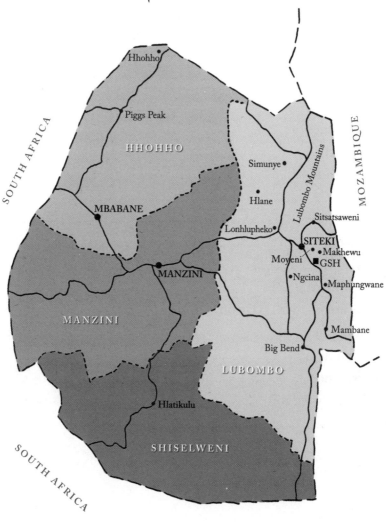

Map of Swaziland

Hhohho

Piggs Peak

HHOHHO

SOUTH AFRICA

Simunye

Hlane

Lubombo Mountains

MOZAMBIQUE

MBABANE

Sitsatsaweni

Lonhlupheko

SITEKI
Makhewu

Moyeni

GSH

MANZINI

Ngcina

Maphungwane

MANZINI

Mambane

Big Bend

LUBOMBO

Hlatikulu

SOUTH AFRICA

SHISELWENI

■ GSH = Good Shepherd Hospital

Contents

I wept as *Vula Bevalile* settled into the deepest recesses of my soul.

All too often in this fast-paced world as we try to maximise our efforts, time dictates that we treat our patients and each other with a 'hit and run' approach. While as healthcare providers, objectivising the experience may seemingly make one more efficient, it also removes the humanity from this service to others.

Within the pages of this book, Maithri teaches us to pause, to take the time to gaze into the eyes of those who are suffering. Their eyes are portals to beautiful souls that are but temporarily housed in fractured bodies.

Vula Bevalile teaches us to treat each suffering patient as a loved one. In feeling the pain, the loneliness, and the fear of those suffering, we become loved as we love.

I have been forever touched by this transformational master 'peace'.

DR TERRY A. GORDON
Retired Cardiologist, American Heart Association National
Physician of the Year, and author of *No Storm Lasts Forever*

After I read *Vula Bevalile: Letters from a Young Doctor,* I was stunned. I remember lifting my head up from the book and thinking, 'How can life just carry on? Everyone I know must know about this work.' Some months later I was fortunate enough to meet Dr Maithri Goonetilleke for coffee, and I had a similar reaction: I walked out into the street and thought, 'How can people just be going about their ordinary business? Everyone should help this doctor and his work.'

What this one young doctor has done for humankind in seven years is more than most of us do in many lifetimes. While the average young doctor was worrying about his or her career, mortgage, or holidays, Maithri was concerned about the best way to help the most disadvantaged people in the world help themselves. Utilising a holistic approach and economic, social, and cultural solutions, Maithri and the foundation he has established, Possible Dreams International, have changed lives—not only in Swaziland but also amongst the readership of this book. Sometimes 'impossible' is actually 'possible'.

A/Prof Katrina Watson
MBBS FRACP MPH
Alumni Relations Coordinator, Melbourne Medical School

FOREWORD

Wayne Dyer

The book you hold in your hands is a treasure, written by a man who has dedicated his life to bringing healing and love to those who are so desperately in need of such attention. These beautiful letters express a burning desire on the part of a physician to reach out and live from a place of divine love.

In a recent public lecture, where I was speaking before several thousand people in a theatre in Melbourne, Australia, I was rendered virtually helpless by the surfacing of a nerve pain in my neck that literally brought me to my knees and forced me to temporarily leave the stage in severe immobilizing pain. Maithri was in the audience that day to listen in person to the man whose writing he had first read as a young teenager.

Maithri immediately rushed to my aid, assisted me in being able to return to the stage and complete my presentation, and then spent the rest of the day driving and accompanying me to the emergency room at a local hospital. It was at that point that the integrity and the vision of this young doctor were made evident. Maithri did for me what he has done for so many desperate people in need, which you will read about in this stellar book.

In the days that I spent in Melbourne, Maithri was totally devoted to my healing: he made arrangements for me to meet with the top medical specialists in Australia; he garnered prescriptions to abate the excruciating pain that persisted in my neck and upper back; he and his sister came to my hotel room and literally serenaded me, singing a spectacular duet version of 'Amazing Grace' that truly brought tears to my eyes and healing to my wounded body; and he arranged for me to have a home-cooked meal with his entire family, prepared in traditional Sri Lankan style by his mother—an evening that remains seared in my mind as one of the peak experiences of my life. In the same fashion that Maithri writes about here in *Vula Bevalile*, reaching out to those in need in rural Swaziland where disease and poverty run rampant, he expressed loving kindness to me in a land far away from my home.

Maithri has referred to me as his teacher and mentor, and as an inspiration for his commitment to living his life as a spiritual seeker and servant to those who live in truly impoverished conditions. As I write this brief foreword to this remarkable book I wanted you to know that the man who wrote these profoundly touching letters, has become his mentor's mentor and teacher. He is *my* inspiration. He is as close to an example of someone living at divine love, a state that I aspire to myself, as anyone I have ever encountered. The inner mantra of the ego-directed man is, 'What's in it for me?', while the inner mantra of the realised being is, 'How may I serve?'. Maithri lives his life every day reaching out in service, whether it be to a lonely HIV-infected child in rural Africa, a homeless grandmother living with little hope in her heart, or a visiting author from America writhing in pain on a stage in Australia.

I have always attempted to teach each of my eight children to, above all else, suspend their egos and reach out and serve others in any way that they are able. The man who wrote this book personifies that spiritual truth, and I am honoured to introduce him to you as a man, a physician, and a spiritual servant who truly walks his talk. The great Persian poet known as Hafiz, once observed, 'Even after all this time, the Sun never says to the Earth, "You owe me"; just think what a love like that can do, it lights up the whole sky.' This is the love that Maithri Goonetilleke writes about and lives. May you shed this illuminating essence to someone in need as you experience the heartfelt letters contained in this masterful collection written by my brother from another mother.

Wayne Dyer is an internationally renowned author and speaker in the field of self-development. He has written over thirty books, has created many audio programs and videos, and has appeared on thousands of television and radio shows. He holds a Doctorate in Educational Counselling and was an associate professor at St. John's University in New York.

INTRODUCTION

Paul A. Komesaroff

Maithri Goonetilleke's book of letters and reflections about his experiences in Swaziland is deceptively simple. On the face of it, these are uncomplicated stories of encounters of a doctor from Australia who travels to a town in Swaziland to provide medical care. He is confronted by the poverty he encounters but impressed by the openness, generosity, and dignity of the people.

He comes to treat their illnesses, to dress their wounds. He lacks resources but does his best in one of the poorest countries in the world, where life expectancy at birth is less than fifty years, where more than a quarter of the adult population is infected with HIV, where ten per cent of the children are orphans, where more than two-thirds of the population live below the poverty line, where infant mortality rates are ten times—and maternal mortality forty times—what is regarded as acceptable in Australia. He comes to a place where one could be forgiven for responding with despair, with resignation, with a sense that the task is too great, the poverty too extreme, the suffering too intense, for there to be any hope of making a significant impact.

As we read Dr Goonetilleke's book we are compelled to wonder why he does it, why someone would go to work in a country as poverty-stricken and oppressed as Swaziland, where the suffering is so intense and the pain so severe. We cannot avoid asking what it is that drives someone to leave the easy comfort of his own home, the convenience of computers, air conditioners, microwave ovens, televisions with remote controls and other gadgets, of easy access to restaurants, bars, nightclubs, movie theatres, swimming pools. We wonder why someone sets aside his own pleasure to put himself at the service of others. We ask why someone will spend his own money, forgo a secure and predictable future for himself and his family, and put himself at physical risk, to provide care and assistance to people who have, and expect, none of those things.

This book does not give us the answers to those questions. But it does give us a few clues, and it provides a few insights into the rewards that Maithri, the doctor, experiences. It shows us that, whatever the motivations that drive him, what he finds is deep wealth, pure goodness, kindness, delicacy, and sensitivity. An elderly woman expresses her gratitude with a nod of her head. When after a

18

month of pleading an orphanage is found to allow two small children to escape the danger of sexual abuse, the neighbours express thanks for their good fortune. A young woman with a debilitating neurological condition shows her enjoyment of a few spoons of yoghurt. An old grandmother at the end of her life acknowledges with a smile that her pain has at last been assuaged.

We go to foreign places and we encounter ourselves, and our pasts and futures. We come into contact with different cultures and different customs, which throw our own habits and assumptions into question. We come with our prejudices and our expectations, and we find ourselves questioning ourselves, and our own goals and values.

This book opens up such challenges to us. It calls on us to think again, to ask ourselves what we are doing in our own lives and why. Reading it, we are compelled to review what it is that propels us forward and to reflect on our own values, aspirations, and expectations, on what we ourselves are spending our lives struggling for. This book confronts us with the need to question the meaning of those gadgets and goods for the acquisition of which we devote so much of our energies.

This is not to say that life in a developed country is less virtuous, that consumer goods are of no value, or that somehow, because our children do not die at birth, battle with the effects of malnutrition or widespread social dislocation, our own lives lack moral content. Nor is it to say that people living ordinary lives in wealthy countries do not suffer, or are less passionate or compassionate, than those who endure rougher and more rudimentary material circumstances.

Indeed, it allows us to recognise the exact opposite: to understand that our own lives too are full of pathos, that we ourselves also confront pain and suffering and have the capacity to offer hope and care and love. This book does not presume to tell us that poor people are purer or better or more honest, or even that people like Maithri, who expose themselves to privation and danger to care for those in need, are better or more wholesome or more moral people. It does not diminish the force or value of our own lives. It does not mark out an alternative path that we should all follow. There are no judgments in this book. It simply asks us questions. It calls on us to suspend our own daily lives for a moment and reflect. Every story is a parable, a metaphor, a window on the people of Siteki, and on ourselves.

There is in these pages no detailed analysis of the predicament of Africa or of the reason for the failure of countless attempts to stimulate development or to stem the devastation of the AIDS epidemic. There is no criticism of the world's inaction or neglect as the people of Swaziland have languished in tragedy. But there is hope and inspiration, pathos, generosity, and a passion about whose origins we can only wonder.

This partly explains why Dr Goonetilleke's book is so compelling. As foreign to many of us as the people in it may be, as different as their cultures, as far away from our own concerns are their problems, we can understand their joys, we can easily share in their laughter, we can cry with them in their pain. We discover that their foreignness is really only on the surface. Remarkably, we find that, like Maithri, we are bound to them in ways that we cannot define.

Mother Teresa is said to have remarked, while applying, with her bare hands, a balm to the open wound of a patient with leprosy, that while the balm was to heal the wound, it was the hand that was healing the soul. Maithri's book brings home to us the deep wisdom in this statement: it shows us that treating illnesses and dressing wounds is a complicated business that ultimately returns us to the fundamental connection that binds us all together, to the bond from which none of us can escape.

––––––––––

PAUL A. KOMESAROFF
Professor of Medicine and Director, Centre for Ethics in Medicine and Society, Monash University, Melbourne, Australia
Executive Director of Global Reconciliation, Australia

PREFACE

The fulfilment of a promise

Since my first visit to Swaziland in 2005, my life has been transformed. I still remember sitting on a little plane from Johannesburg bound for Manzini that very first time, blissfully unaware that my life would forever be altered by the people I would encounter and the depth of human joy and suffering I would witness in the years to come. There would be no going back.

At that time, Swaziland was a country with the lowest life expectancy and the highest prevalence of HIV/AIDS anywhere in the world. In the town where I worked, it seemed easier to find a coffin salesman than a grocery store. According to the UNDP's Human Development Report 2006, a child born in Swaziland in 2004 had a life expectancy of just thirty-one years, due primarily to the prevalence of HIV/AIDS. As a result of soaring death rates, one third of all Swazi children,[1] a staggering ten percent of the entire Swazi population, were orphaned.

The movement of change is slow, but inexorable. Since my first visit, increased access to anti-retroviral medication for HIV-infected patients has led to a substantial increase in life expectancy, up to fifty years by June 2011.[2] However, even in 2012, UNAIDS data still showed Swaziland having the highest prevalence of AIDS of any country in the world.[3] There is still work to be done.

This book contains my letters written from rural Swaziland over my first seven years as a medical practitioner there. For this updated edition, I am delighted to have been able to add two new stories from my most recent trip to Swaziland. I am grateful to Prof Paul Kommesaroff for writing the original introduction, which still appears in this second edition, and honoured to have Dr Wayne Dyer, A/Prof Katrina Watson, and Dr Terry Gordon graciously endorse this new edition.

The promise I made during my very first visit to Swaziland was to return to Australia to tell the stories of those humble and almost unfathomably courageous people. This book is my attempt.

Maithri Goonetilleke

---

1 CSO. (2007). 2006-2007 Swaziland Demographic and Health Survey. Mbabane: Government of the Kingdom of Swaziland.
2 www.who.int/countries/swz/en/
3 UNAIDS World AIDS Day Report 2012

Loneliness

It's not uncommon to hear a tourist say of Swaziland, 'It's such a beautiful country, I can't imagine there being poverty here.'

The long, black road that winds from Mbabane down towards Lonhlupheko and Simunye affords spectacular views of a country cradled by mountains. Rolling hills rise on every side like green-eyed friends, and, as you pass well-built towns like Manzini, seeing the sumptuous houses of the elite that stud the roadside, you might be forgiven for believing that perhaps the iron fist of poverty had fled this beautiful land.

And yet the fact remains that forty percent of the Swazi population live in extreme poverty. * It is exactly those 'forty percent' that the tourists don't see. The vast majority of poor people live in what is known as 'rural Swaziland', away from the tarred road—in places where houses are made of mud and sticks and lives are lived on the brink.

One such mud-and-stick house resides at the bottom of a red-dust hill in the rural town of Maphungwane. It's a tiny place, comprised of just one room, no more than a few metres in diameter. Its sole inhabitant is an elderly *gogo*, a grandmother, named Anna.

Anna warms the interior of her little house with her gentle voice and a singular humility that dwells in her brown eyes. She loves to sing, and often sits on the floor beside her old wooden door singing songs of her childhood. Her voice is so soft that it usually goes unheard.

Anna is all alone.

Several years ago, Anna lost the use of both her legs, and ever since she has spent the most part of each day seated on the dirt floor of her little room. When she wants to go somewhere, she crawls on her hands and knees.

On a recent visit we learned that small holes had developed in the corners of Anna's house and ceiling. We counted twelve holes in total.

At night when darkness would fall across the Lubombo Mountains, and she lay down to sleep, the holes would become open invitations, nocturnal gateways, for an army of mice.

'*Dokotela*, when the sun sets, I hear them coming,' she told me. 'They come through the roof, through the floor. Ten. Fifteen. Twenty of them.'

And once inside, the mice would begin to nibble upon her almost immobile feet.

'I used to be terrified at first,' she said. 'But now I am used to them. Now when they come and eat my feet, it simply reminds me that I have no one. If I was to cry out for help, who would come to help me? No one knows that I am here.'

I stood in her little one-room home and tried to imagine the horror that *Gogo* Anna was enduring; what must it be like to feel your cries, your voice, being swallowed by the darkness?

So, as the yellow sun traced its path across the sky, we went to work. We had a wonderful team of workers: Beki, Matron Zwane, Jacque, as well as members of the local community and some friends from America, who weren't afraid to get their hands dirty. Some of us went in to Siteki and purchased some essential items for *Gogo* while the rest of the team started work on transforming her home.

Over the course of twenty-four hours we cleaned, mixed cement to fill the holes, and laid down coverings for the floor. We threw out the mouse-eaten mattress and blanket that *Gogo* had been lying on for all those years, and replaced them with new ones.

We also laid down rat poison, and over the next few days we collected the corpses of no less than twenty adult mice.

Today I went to re-visit *Gogo* and found her sleeping in her new bed under the red blanket which we had purchased for her.

While I sat with her, I remembered something else she had said during our very first meeting. '*Dokotela*,' she had said, 'I have pain everywhere. Pain in my eyes. In my fingernails. Everywhere.'

So today I asked, '*Yini inkinga, Gogo. Kubuhlungu kuphi,*' to see if she still had any pain.

She replied with a gentle smile, 'No pain. No pain.'

As Matron Zwane sat down beside her, *Gogo* Anna started to sing.

From Siteki with love,

Maithri

---

* www.unicef.org/infobycountry/swaziland_statistics.html

LOVE

Something remarkable happens when Lindiwe smiles.

Maybe if I was a better photographer I could capture it—the whole world softening in a single moment.

Lindiwe is fifteen years old with light-flecked eyes and caramel skin. I have known her for about three years now. She suffers from a progressive neurological disorder that has never been fully diagnosed.

Since birth Lindiwe has had a steadily increasing weakness, whereby she has developed flaccid paralysis of her limbs. At times she is unable to even lift her head from her pillow. We think there may be a lesion in her spinal cord, but her family has never had the resources to obtain CT or MRI imaging of her spine to confirm that suspicion.

During a recent visit to the little homestead, full of children, where she lives, we found her shivering under a tiny, dirty blanket, breathing very rapidly. She had contracted a strain of pneumonia that was too virulent for treatment with oral antibiotics.

We transferred her to hospital where she began receiving antibiotics intravenously. She has been making a steady recovery there for several days now.

Every night after work, I drop in to visit Lindiwe. She cannot move her head to acknowledge my presence in the room. But she smiles, with a deep sincerity and gentle grace that never fails to move me.

In the past few days, Lindiwe has seen two young women die in the bed next to her. Both were infected with HIV, and both suffered greatly.

When I sit down on the wooden stool by her bed, we talk about her day. Due to what we believe to be a progressive weakness of her laryngeal muscles, Lindiwe speaks very softly and tires quickly.

Something that few people know about Lindiwe is that she loves yoghurt—thick, apricot yoghurt.

On my visits I always try to remember to bring a small tub. I lift her head from the mattress with one hand, and with a spoon borrowed from the hospital kitchen I feed her a little yoghurt before bedtime.

She savours each spoonful, and swallows slowly and carefully before nodding her head to tell me to continue.

When she has had her fill, she whispers, 'Enough.' Then I wipe her mouth with the towel that sits by her bed and ask, 'How was it, my friend?'

Lindiwe smiles broadly and gently, as if to say, it was good. The joy on her face illuminates the dimly lit hospital room.

It has become our little ritual, and I look forward to it at the end of each day.

Sitting together in that darkened corner of the female ward, I feed her, and in her own innocent way, without realising it, she feeds me.

From Siteki with love,

Maithri

Gratitude

Early one misty morning, Matron Anna Zwane and I ventured out in a borrowed truck to deliver some food parcels to *gogos* in deep need out in some of the rural communities of Lubombo.

There are few people in this world who I revere more than *gogos*, the Swazi grandmothers, who I have come to know so well.

As the AIDS pandemic claims the lives of increasing numbers of women of child-bearing age and young men, a legacy of lonely little hands and feet is left behind; they are the ones we call AIDS orphans. Approximately one third of all Swazi children have lost both their mother and father to AIDS.

Gogos form an integral part of Swazi society, and upon the death of their own children they will often take their grandchildren, or even other unfortunate children, into their homes.

Many *gogos* are frail and unemployed, making their ability to care for a throng of prepubescent children all the more remarkable.

One of our initiatives is to support *gogos* who have taken large numbers of orphans into their care, often as many as ten or twenty children each. We assist with cultivation of gardens, income generation, and the provision of a monthly food supplement, until such time as they can provide for themselves.

When we visited *Gogo* Josephine in the grassy, rural community of Moyeni, it was for the very first time.

'*Gogo* Josephine is blind,' Matron explained as we drove. She described a series of family deaths and painful life events that had left *Gogo* with over ten grandchildren in her care. As we reached her house, it seemed that *Gogo* Josephine was waiting for someone.

Grey walking stick in hand, a white and blue cloth wrapped around her head, she sat silently outside her crumbling home. Her face was beautiful—wrinkled it seemed by the mingling of time, love, and tears.

As we spoke to her, Josephine began to share stories of her life, and the lessons she had learned along the way. There was dignity in her presence, and a gentle, unpretentious wisdom about her. I asked her where it came from. She explained it derived from the daily washing of clothes, the harvesting of maize, and the feeding of little mouths.

We explained why we had come—that in addition to helping the family to cultivate a garden we had a few practical things to share with them.

Anna read out the list: five kilograms of peanuts; another five of sugar; ten kilograms of rice; fifty kilograms of maize meal; a kilo of soap; ten white candles; and five grey storm-blankets.

Blind *Gogo* Josephine turned to us—not seeing us, yet seeing us at the same time. She began to weep. 'Can I touch them?' she asked in tender siSwati.

One by one, Matron took the inanimate objects out of the truck and held them out for *Gogo* Josephine to hold.

We watched as she caressed them, adored them, enfolded them with her warmth. She softly raised the long, green bar of soap to her face like the hand of a lover. She embraced the bag of maize meal like the shoulders of a child. And then she took the dull, grey storm-blanket and stroked it with a reverence and mindfulness which I'm sure a storm-blanket is not accustomed. Then she began to pray, in tremulous siSwati: '*Siyabonga, siyabonga, siyabonga.*' She was saying, 'Thank you.'

'How she could be so grateful?' I asked myself. Josephine had lost everything: her husband, her children, her mobility, her vision. Why would she cry, 'Thank you,' for a bar of soap, a portion of rice, and a dull, grey storm-blanket? And yet, as she continued to talk to us about her life, I began to realise, that for Josephine, gratitude was more than a fleeting experience. Gratitude was a way.

It seems there are many roads through adversity. Some paths attempt to remove us from reality, while others harden the heart in order to protect from further pain. But in Swaziland, there is another way which I have witnessed on a regular basis. It has to do with focusing on the little things we have and being grateful, even in the midst of scarcity and adversity. Often it's not expressed in words, and yet it is manifestly apparent—in the laughter of children on a swing made of rags or playing with a soccer ball made out of plastic bags, in the smiles of women carrying giant burdens on their heads, and in the men suddenly dancing with each other when they are working in the fields.

That was Josephine's path—a path frequently intersected by death, illness, and worsening disability. Many times it seemed Josephine had seen the fracturing of hope, and yet her response was to pick up the splinters and say, 'Thank you'.

From Siteki with love,

Maithri

FISHING

In the throbbing heart of Siteki, I'm seated in the little veterinary clinic that doubles as an internet café. I've never actually witnessed any animals being treated here, nor for that matter anyone who claims to be a veterinarian. Perhaps the name is merely an interesting English embellishment, as is the idea of calling it an internet café when you consider the number of determined clients, like me, who sit frustrated and bathed in sweat as they attempt for the nineteenth time to transmit two simple sentences via email before the fragile internet connection stops again indefinitely.

Outside, the air is alive with red dust and the strident calls from densely peopled buses and street vendors. It is summer in Swaziland, the wet season, and the recent, welcomed rain has turned many of the roads to mud.

Yesterday, we played our familiar game of 'sardines', which involves packing several robust nurses and one young doctor into a small but steadfast vehicle we lovingly call our 'truck'. It is actually a large four-wheel-drive with a covered utility-type tray at the back in which medicines, and occasionally people, are transported. Yesterday, it seemed that the only thing more densely peopled than our vehicle was the number of patients on our list.

After treating several women and children with opportunistic infections secondary to HIV, and a brief lunch break taken under the shade of an acacia tree, the team arrived at the foot of a tall and inhospitable hill. It was strewn with jagged rocks and overgrown with wild grasses. There was no road in sight.

However, knowing that we needed to get to the top to call on our next patient, our intrepid driver persevered. The truck careened, groaned, and occasionally snarled as it awkwardly navigated the rocky slope.

Eventually we reached the summit, and in blind faith we opened the creaky doors of our truck, cautiously stepping out into an endless sea of wild yellow grass.

'Careful of mambas!' I said, partially to myself. A snake bite was the last thing any of us needed up there.

After unloading the truck we carried food packs and medical supplies to a little, thatched mud hut standing just a few metres away.

'It's been some time since we were last here,' *Make* Maposa exclaimed. 'The man who lives here is very sick, *Dokotela*. Very sick.'

As we stepped into the hut, I understood what she meant.

Lying naked on a dirty, rat-eaten mattress, alone in the darkness, was a man in the end stages of HIV. He was severely malnourished—no more than a skeleton covered in a thin garment of brown skin. The contour and arc of every rib was clearly visible, palpable. Next to him was a putrid pool of his own wastes.

Since the onset of AIDS, his brain had become secondarily infected with toxoplasmosis, which had in turn precipitated a stroke. He could not move his left side.

As I examined him, I wondered how long it had been since anyone had touched him.

Make Maposa told me more about his plight. 'There is a daughter who comes each evening after work. She has her own family. They live at the bottom of the hill. She comes each night, feeds him, and changes this bowl of his wastes. But you can see *Dokotela*, he is hungry.'

That was a profound understatement.

We gave him an orange. He took it in his skeletal hands and devoured it. We took out a bag of maize meal and the nurses mixed it with some milk into porridge. Within seconds it was gone.

We shared the little gifts we had brought, leaving a toothbrush, nappies, and some simple medicines to help treat the incessant diarrhoea that can be so dehumanising in stage four HIV.

After he had finished his porridge he looked at each one of us, holding our gaze for a moment, his eyes swollen with tears, trying to convey something that he did not have the strength to explain. In one tremulous motion he lifted a brittle hand and thanked us, '*Siyabonga.*'

I remembered the old catchcry, which most of us who study international health would be proud to have pinned to our lapels: 'Give a man a fish, and you will feed him for a day. Teach a man to fish, and you will feed him for a lifetime.'

That catchcry resonates because it is true. Change needs to be sustainable. Empowerment and engagement with individuals and communities should ultimately involve helping those in need to assist themselves.

But this man, with the lowest possible CD4 count and a palliative diagnosis, was far too weak to even take hold of the fishing rod, much less learn how to fish.

So it was his community who would have to do the fishing for him. We sought out his daughter, and helped her to cultivate a garden to give the man a sustainable food source. Then we left him with enough 'fish' for the month, till we came to see him again.

There is a story about a sparrow, which my father told me once.

The sparrow was lying on a gravel road, with his little, scrawny legs facing the open sky.

A horseman came riding along, and seeing the sparrow, alighted from his horse.

He said, 'Little sparrow, are you hurt? Why are you lying there so awkwardly, face up to the sky?'

To those words, the sparrow replied, 'I have heard, that sometime today, the sky will fall.'

The horseman laughed and said, 'And you think you can keep it from falling with those little legs?'

The sparrow shrugged his shoulders and said, 'My friend, I will do what I can.'

Sometimes here in Siteki, this little hamlet filled with pain, it seems that the sky is falling.

We do what we can.

From Siteki with love,

Maithri

AIDS

It was midday. The wild, orange sun burnt a slow arc through the southern sky, as our truck thrashed its way through a field of yellow grass, buffeting towards the home of our next patient.

As three Swazi nurses and I stepped down from the vehicle it seemed as though the cement house that we were visiting had been abandoned. The windows were shattered; the doors were barred and barricaded.

'*Sanibonani ekhaya,*' Anna Zwane's voice, rich and deep, rang through the homestead, as she called through the window asking if anyone was home.

After a moment's pause we began to turn to leave, when suddenly I heard something:

Music.

Soft, and crackling like cellophane, it was a melody, playing on a radio inside the shuttered house.

Sensing that someone must be inside or nearby, I wondered if the patient we had come to see had collapsed or was too unwell to walk to the door. We decided to find a way into the house and discovered a corner entrance. Suddenly darkness surrounded us.

Each footstep we made was shrouded in shadows. The musty scent of sickness hung mutely in the air.

We came to a dimly lit hall, and there, as our eyes grew accustomed to the darkness, we saw a young man standing silently. We persuaded him to come into the kitchen where there was light streaming through a window. Bare-chested and weak, he wore only a pair of dark-green cotton pants. The sadness in his eyes was unmistakeable.

The nurses and I engaged him in conversation. We found out that he was hiding from his community. He wanted no one to see his 'wound'.

After asking the others to step out of the room, I said, as gently as I could, 'Show me, brother.'

He removed his pants, and there on his right leg was a giant, fungating tumour. Extending from his hip all the way down to his toes, it looked as though his skin was bubbling up underneath the pressure of the giant mass that had overtaken his leg.

There was infection too, with pus oozing, and a smell so pungent that I had to hold my breath just to get close enough to continue my examination.

I recognised the type of tumour. It was an uncontrolled form of Kaposi's sarcoma (KS), a cancer caused by a virus which in medical circles is described as an 'AIDS defining illness', a hallmark of the end stages of HIV.

Normally when we see KS lesions, they are blotchy, palpable outcrops on the skin. But here was a case so advanced that it had partially obstructed the clearance vessels of the body, the lymphatic system—resulting in grotesque swelling from lymphoedema, skin break down, and multiple fungating lesions.

I asked him whether he knew he had AIDS.

'Of course, *Dokotela*.'

'Have you been to hospital?'

He told me that when he was twenty he fell in love with a girl. They had been together for a few years when he

47

started to become sick. One day his leg began to swell, gradually becoming bigger and uglier, until the skin bubbled and came away; eventually it began oozing with infection.

His girlfriend left him, he lost his job, and his community shunned him. People threw stones through his windows. He was suddenly isolated and viscerally alone.

One day he walked the forty kilometres to hospital. It must have been terribly painful. He was told that he had AIDS, and was given some medicine and asked to come back each month for his 'refills'.

AIDS medication is very effective but can cause significant nausea. Because he had no food to take with his medicine, every time he ingested his pills he would vomit. What is more, the journey to hospital was physically too much for him to make each month. And the bus fare was at least fifteen rand, about two Australian dollars, and that was fifteen rand that he simply didn't have.

So he resigned himself to his fate—barred all the doors and windows, shut out the light, and prayed each day for his God to take him home.

Like most diseases, HIV/AIDS does not exist in isolation. In Swaziland, and in so much of sub-Saharan Africa, there is an insidious and deeply rooted cycle involving extreme poverty that can undermine our best efforts to help alleviate suffering. We cannot make real change in the AIDS pandemic without addressing the abject poverty in which so many patients live.

So many times I ask myself, 'What is the point of giving free medicine if a patient cannot afford the bus fare to obtain it, or the food to take with it?'

After we cleaned his wounds and administered antibiotic and antifungal therapy, we spoke at length about how he might be able to help himself. We talked about how important it was to take his antiviral medication every single day and that we would need to find ways for him to get to hospital and to have a sustainable food source.

Anna Zwane suggested bringing the community together to build a small chicken coop and a vegetable garden as food sources, with the potential of also generating an income.

'Let's do it, this week, Matron!' I suggested enthusiastically.

Smiling and taking me aside, Anna Zwane said with deep respect, respect that a Swazi elder does not normally need to pay to someone younger like me, 'No, young *Dokotela*, that is not the way.'

She explained that she would speak to the *Indvuna* and organise a community meeting. There she would address them on bended knee, and, with her voice full of grace, implore them to be kind to the young man—to gather around him and support him. Then the chicken coop and the garden will be easily achieved.

As we were about to leave, I asked him if there was anything else we could do for him at the moment.

'Come and see me again, *Dokotela*. Just come see me again.'

We promised that we would.

From Siteki with love,

Maithri

A FEW LITTLE ANTS

We stepped from the truck to a sea of ants that seemed to be pouring out of every crack in the dry earth. Matron Zwane, Beki, Thembi, and I gazed across a silent multitude of insects surging towards a tired, precariously placed homestead.

Gogo Dlamini lives in that homestead. Her beautiful, ebony skin and tender eyes conceal a life of visceral hardship. Being poor and without education, she settled for a plot of land on the barren outskirts of her community. Her home, now a mud-and-stick structure, was perched upon a dry, rocky outcrop. From up there, everything is inaccessible. From there, everything is far away.

I first met *Gogo* Dlamini in 2005. Her little two-year-old grandson was in a critical condition at the time, suffering from severe malnutrition, tuberculosis, and acute vitamin A deficiency. Vitamin A is found in foods like carrots, pumpkin, and green leafy vegetables, but *Gogo* had no food sources with Vitamin A to help her provide for her grandchild—no carrots, no other vegetables. In fact, on many days *Gogo* had no food at all.

Due to a deficiency in micronutrients, the delicate structures of one of her grandson's eyes had begun to break down: he had developed a deep corneal ulcer, and a condition known as keratomalacia. His right eye was bright-red and swollen. Around his eye he had developed burn-like marks that were a consequence of infection. His vitamin deficiency was so severe that at the age of two he was declared blind in his right eye.

Since that time *Gogo* had struggled not only with the health of her grandchildren, but her own health. She had recurrent episodes of tuberculosis, and her HIV infection had progressed into the more advanced stages. She now had six children to look after, and no income.

I watched from a distance, still dusting ants off my shoes in the blinding sun, as Beki and Matron Zwane greeted *Gogo* with a smile. *Gogo* was sitting on a large, grey rock surrounded by thorn bushes.

Beki is a quiet young man who grew up in rural Makhewu. He has a deep connection to his culture and his people. When he speaks, his voice is soft, and he carries himself with dignity.

'*Gogo*, how is the ARV treatment going?' Beki said in siSwati, asking about her AIDS medication.

'Not well,' came her reply. 'We have no food, so I must take the pills on an empty stomach. It makes me vomit. Now I have decided to cut the pills in half, take one today and one the next day.'

'No, *Make*, no,' Matron Zwane interjected, shaking her head in deep concern.

'*Make*, AIDS is a flood,' Matron continued as she stepped forward. 'Half a pill will not stop the flow. We must find a way for you to take the whole pill every day.'

In a sign of respect, Beki took a half step back to let Matron continue.

'How are the children?' Matron asked.

'Not well. There is a snake in this house, Matron. He lives in the wall and comes out at night. The children are scared.' *Gogo* was clearly upset.

'And there,' *Gogo* pointed to the wall of her mud house. 'You see that hole? The storms are tearing our house down.' A single tear rolled down her face. Embarrassed, she turned away.

In an act of pure instinct, Matron put her hand on *Gogo's* shoulder, speaking in a whispered tone in siSwati.

Beki joined in, his voice and Matron's in tandem now, 'Do not worry, *Make*, we are here to help you, but there is more that is needed than just food and a house. You need to find a way of supporting yourself. Have you thought of any work you could do?'

'I want to grow vegetables and sell them at the market in Maphungwane,' she said as bravely as she could through the tears.

'We will help you, *Make*. Tomorrow we will visit the Community Committee, and we will discuss where the best place to sell your produce would be. We will ask for their advice and the community's support. And as for a new house and help with growing your garden, the team can help.'

I sat on a nearby rock, absorbed by the conversation while trying to ignore the incessant intrusion of ants. They were everywhere. Every few moments I found myself kicking them off my shoes or dusting them from my clothes. 'Get off me!' I thought to myself.

But always my attention returned to *Gogo* as she sat on the rock speaking to the team. Hope was slowly returning to her face.

The ants were all over her. They were crawling up her legs, her hands, even her face and hair. Unlike me, she didn't appear to be the slightest bit irritated by them. She wasn't even moving to wipe them away.

I thought of the many adversities that we had watched her family endure over the years, particularly her own resilience in the face of persistent setbacks. A few little ants were not going to distract her from that moment. Her eyes were fixed on other things.

From Siteki with love,

Maithri

Moments with Matron

Over the years I have met many visiting physicians and health care workers in the little hamlet of Siteki. They come to learn and teach at the hospital on the hill, the Good Shepherd Hospital.

On any given day on the grounds of the Good Shepherd you might see Dr Petros, a surgeon and our senior medical officer, or Dr Joyce Mareverwa, a brilliant Zimbabwean paediatrician walking hand in hand with children from the Paediatric ward. If you wandered to the Outpatient department with its long queue of patients awaiting care, you might meet a family of diligent doctors from the south of India: Dr Koshy who works in Outpatients, Dr Asha in Obstetrics and Gynaecology, and Dr Gladge in the Ear, Nose, and Throat department. Down the long, dark corridors of the hospital you might hear the laughter of Dr Kalungero, a Congolese physician, or encounter Dr Jono Pons, the most extraordinary eye surgeon I have ever known. Jono runs his own department at the Good

Shepherd, and also oversees young medical students from around the world as they learn first-hand the realities of medical practice in Swaziland.

Away from the clinical side of things Dumsile Simelane, the administrator of the hospital, is the strong leader of the hospital. She is a wise Swazi woman who is well versed in Swazi tradition and custom; she is an excellent resource when I want to make sure that I'm doing things the Swazi way.

The hospital remains the major health care centre for the entire Lubombo region of Swaziland. When I first came to Swaziland the hospital was quite literally overflowing: patients were sleeping under beds, in corridors, and in waiting areas; there was simply not enough room to cater for the volume and intensity of ill people that poured through the doors on a daily basis.

It was at the Good Shepherd, in the absence of fancy analytical equipment like CT scans and MRIs, that I learned about the value of my stethoscope and about basic clinical skills. It was also there that I learned my most important lessons about community-based medicine, home-based care, and the insidious cycle of poverty and disease. The doctors and nurses at this hospital have been my mentors, teachers, and friends.

Perhaps the most significant of all those teachers has been Matron Anna Zwane. I remember the day that two volunteers came to Swaziland from Australia and were held up in customs. When I went into customs to discuss the situation with immigration officials, I found that the problem was that the volunteers had brought a suitcase full of soft toys with them, to distribute to children at the orphan care points.

The officials weren't convinced of the volunteers' intentions, however, and had refused entry on the grounds that the toys might be being brought into the country to sell for profit. I did my best to explain the purpose of their visit and to vouch for their integrity, but it seemed to no avail. Then I happened to mention that the head of our team was Matron Anna Zwane. The expression on the face of the sternest officer softened in an instant.

'Matron Zwane?' he said. 'She sat by mother when she was dying in hospital. She visited us every day for a year afterwards.' Then he motioned that the volunteers could go, and said, 'Give her my love.'

Each day I have the privilege of learning from Matron. As we drive across the rugged Swazi countryside, she tells me stories of her life: how she lectured in Kenya, worked in Malawi, about her decades as Matron of the Good Shepherd Hospital, and the experience of being called out of retirement to assist with the emergency response to the AIDS crisis. We talk of Swazi kings and queens, of her great respect for tradition and culture, and the ways she has witnessed well-intentioned volunteers regularly violate Swazi customs.

Her navigational senses are extraordinary. In rural Swaziland there are no street signs or house numbers, and often no roads, yet she remembers the exact whereabouts of each of the people she tends to.

'Left at the tree ... No, not that one, *Dokotela*, this one!'

'But Matron, there is no road here ...'

'My son, why do you always need a road to get to where you are going?'

It was on one of our regular trips into rural communities that I first met Zanele. Zanele is a tall, statuesque young lady who lives in the Makhewu community. When her husband died of AIDS she was left with six children, all under the age of ten. She was unemployed, uneducated, and felt entirely overwhelmed by the prospect of looking after her children on her own.

Her initial response was to run away. She ran to South Africa leaving behind the children. While the team worried desperately about what would happen, Matron established a sense of calm, 'She will return. She is a good girl, she's just heart-broken. We will talk to *Make* Bhembe, a leader in the Makhewu community, and to the *Indvuna*, to make sure the children are safe.'

At meetings of the local elders and community leaders, there is no one who is more comfortable. Matron knows when to speak and what to say; she knows the tone of voice to be used and the gestures that will be understood.

Sure enough, as we went about the business of following Matron's instructions, Zanele returned to Makhewu. We organised a meeting with Zanele and our team. I'll never forget Matron's gentleness that day. As Zanele wept, Matron held her head in her hands, saying very few words. Every day for several months Matron and *Make* Bhembe would sit with Zanele in the shade beside her little hut and talk about mothering and the difficulties so many other Swazi women who have also lost their husbands have faced.

Over the two years that followed the relationship between Matron and Zanele deepened. I could see the gratitude and respect in Zanele's eyes whenever she saw Matron approaching. Slowly but surely Zanele found her strength.

When we brought our builders in to build a house for her, Zanele was already planting her first crops of maize. She also built a chicken coop with sticks that she had cut from the forest nearby.

Soon afterwards she found a child-minding job, and her crop had yielded so much maize that it was almost too much to store.

Today, Zanele helps other young women in her community who are going through similar crises that she herself had been through and overcome.

'She had the ability all along,' Matron Zwane tells me. 'All I did was reveal it to her.'

From Siteki with love,

Maithri

Advocacy

It is June in Lubombo and the aloe is in bloom. Almost everywhere I look I see its fiery orange fingers gently reaching for the sky.

Recently *Make* Bhembe, a friend and leader in the Makhewu community, paid me a visit. She was very concerned about two little children in her community and asked me whether I could see them.

I first met *Make* Bhembe at the Makhewu Care Point for orphans and vulnerable children. In Swaziland, care points are structures where orphaned or vulnerable children can go for a meal each day, and for informal education. Some of the happiest days of my life have been spent at the Makhewu Care Point, playing games, blowing bubbles, and dancing with the kids. There is an irrepressible spirit in so many of the children in rural communities; it is an unfettered joy in the simple things of life.

Yet on the day I walked with *Make* Bhembe up the narrow, brown-dust road that gently winds from the Makhewu Care Point to the house where the two little ones resided, I knew something was seriously amiss.

'There are two children here,' she explained, 'a three-year-old boy and a two-year-old girl. Their young mother had AIDS and died six months ago. Their father is a security guard who works the night shift in Manzini, one hour away from Makhewu. He is rarely with the children, and all night the children are alone. They have no food. They have only one set of clothes each that I see them in every day. They are always frightened.'

As we walked into the homestead, I saw two terrified pairs of brown eyes gazing at us from behind a plank of wood. The children were covered in mud, and their clothes were tattered and filthy.

The hut they were living in was collapsing. It consisted of a few poorly supported sticks in the ground, which reminded me distinctly of a cage.

'How are they eating, *Make*?' I asked.

'They scavenge through the homestead, eating seeds and berries. Sometimes they receive food from neighbours. Usually they don't eat.'

As I looked at their terrified faces, I quietly asked the question to which I almost didn't want to know the answer, 'Are they being hurt?'

'I think so, *Dokotela*. There is a rapist who has been released from the Moyeni prison. People say they see him here in the late hours of the night. We think he may be hurting these children.'

I looked again at the children as they sat silently in their hut. The little boy, at only three years old, was looking after his little sister, chasing flies away from her face as she sat beside him. A quiet and palpable sadness pervaded the homestead.

Finding a food source and clothing for the children would not be an onerous task, but how to make sure that they would not be hurt again, that was the question.

Many times we tried and failed to contact their father. Then one afternoon, while we were with the children, he arrived home suddenly. Tall, young, and imposing, he was wearing a worn green uniform which reminded me of an army sergeant.

Make Bhembe spoke to him with the characteristic respect that a Swazi woman shows to a man. He uttered very few words. Those he did speak were solemn.

'I am a security guard, not a father,' he said.

I sensed that he did not mean it in a callous way. He was speaking his truth. In a place where women do the lion's share of child-rearing, the void that the death of his wife must have left in his family was inestimable. We talked about finding support in the community, to assist him.

When we spoke of the way the children were being hurt while he was at work, he grew silent. He walked away into the thick scrub that grew around the homestead and stood there for several minutes playing with a pebble in his hands. When he returned, his voice was assured. 'Find them a home, please.' With those words he set off. He was catching the bus to his workplace in Manzini.

Each day, for the next month, I started my day outside the social workers office at the Ministry of Health. We had looked for a grandmother to take care of the children, as is the custom in Swazi culture, but it was taking too long, and the children were suffering. I knew there was an orphanage on the other side of Swaziland that took in abused and very vulnerable children, and it not only provided food and clothing, but cared for them in a safe, protected environment, nurturing them with love and a sense of community. Unfortunately for us, places in that orphanage were highly sought after and difficult to obtain.

Every day as we visited the children, I watched them tenderly holding each other's small hands as they walked around their dishevelled homestead together. We asked as many as we could in the Makhewu community to watch over them, to protect them, but I still lay awake most nights worrying about them. *Make* Bhembe and I would return to the homestead most evenings just to make sure they were okay.

For thirty days we pestered the overworked social workers. It became our daily ritual until, finally, I received a call from the Ministry regarding the orphanage—amazingly, the children had been accepted!

The day that the children left Makhewu, *Make* Bhembe dressed them in new clothes. There was a sense of celebration in the air. Neighbours who had engaged in their story came out in force to bid them farewell—finally a safe place, finally a chance to grow up without fear!

'Their mother made this happen, *Dokotela*,' *Make* exclaimed suddenly, explaining her belief that every orphan child had a parent watching over them from beyond. 'Her love is taking them to freedom today.'

As *Make* Bhembe and the children stepped into the car that would take them to the orphanage, I saw out of the corner of my eye a man in green uniform standing by the side of the road. As the car disappeared over the hills of Makhewu, he was watching them too.

From Siteki with love,

Maithri

Vision

It was a hot day. Sweat beaded off my skin onto the stethoscope that hung around my neck like the jet-black arm of an old friend. We had been driving for hours over rocky, red-clay roads lined with maize, thatched huts, and the occasional sunflowers. The challenge at each homestead was not simply to hand out food and medicine but to listen closely and to understand the many reasons why someone was sick. Then we could help them overcome their obstacles to recovery.

There are thirty-four communities that we visit, and that amounts to literally thousands of patients. I don't know how those in the home-based-care team manage to know, not only the directions to every hut or homestead, but the story behind each person, but I am grateful that they do.

Late in the afternoon we came to a poorly constructed stick and stone house with a sheet metal roof. It was hard to believe that it was still standing. I asked the others in the team about the house and the person who lived there.

It was *Make* Maposa who shared with me the story of the man that we had come to see, one of the family members who lived in the house that now stood before us. 'We have heard there is an old man here with untreated TB. He is refusing to come to hospital.'

At the entrance to the homestead we got out of the truck and were greeted by a vibrant, young Swazi man who was one of the breadwinners for the household. He told us to follow him into the home where his family were awaiting us.

As the group was walking towards the house, I stopped short.

Huddled in a lonely corner, just outside the house, I saw an old woman.

'Who is she?' I asked.

'Our *gogo*,' the young man replied.

'Why is she sitting like that?'

'Don't worry about her, *Dokotela*. She is old now and blind. And that is where she always sits.'

'Can she walk?' I added.

'Not really. Only a few steps. We bring her food. We take her in to sleep at night. Her legs don't work anymore.'

I knelt down beside her in the burning sun. The flies swarmed. Looking in her eyes, it was clear that she had bilateral cataracts. I had a hunch that it was visual impairment, as opposed to decreased mobility, that had rendered her unable to walk.

I asked her to stand. She did.

We gave her a walking stick, and asked her to walk if she could. By then other members of her family had gathered around. To her family's surprise, *Gogo* began to walk.

I explained to the family, with *Make* Maposa helping with the translation, 'The reason that *Gogo* cannot see and isn't walking is because she has cataracts covering her eyes. She needs an operation to have them removed. Afterwards, she will be able to see.'

Gogo, whose face had remained downcast for our entire conversation, lifted her face towards the blinding sun, and smiled.

That day, as so often happens, we tended to several people in the one house, when only one person was on our list.

In the developing world, blindness often drastically reduces lifespan. Blindness means that people become unable to fend for themselves in already difficult conditions.

Yet cataract blindness is an eminently treatable condition. The surgery is inexpensive and it takes about twenty minutes. My friend Dr Jonathan Pons does most of the cataract surgeries in Swaziland. He is a person of enormous integrity and deep compassion.

I have stood in Jono's clinic at the Good Shepherd Hospital the day after men and women have had cataract surgery. There will never be words to describe what it is to watch as a group of people, who were blind just twenty-four hours earlier, have the white bandages removed from their eyes and find their sight has been restored.

They start to sing, in groups, in four-and-five-part harmonies, without any prompting.

From Siteki with love,

Maithri

PRESENCE

I sometimes think we underestimate presence.

Twenty-four hours of plane flights and bustling airport terminals can be a stark reminder of how close, and yet how distant, we can be from one another.

I would be one of the first to sing praise to the mobile phone for its singular ability to connect people across the world, but as I sat in a Melbourne Airport departure lounge last evening in the company of a hundred kindred travellers, there was a distinct feeling of disconnectedness. Glancing around me, I became aware that each of us seemed to be walled within our own discrete, invisible cocoon. Sitting in quiet adoration of the phone in our hands, we deftly insulated ourselves from the 'strangers' milling around us.

Often we pay lip-service to the manifest separateness that pervades our communities. Even when it violently rears its head, in the form of psychological and emotional pathology, we brush it off as merely a symptom of the times, a by-product of progress.

As I stepped out of the arrival gate at Matsapha Airport, onto Swazi soil once more, the cocoon of disconnectedness began to lift.

My consistent experience of working in places of extreme material poverty is that an almost counter-intuitive spiritual wealth exists in so many of those places, with such frequency, that it can only be seen as the norm.

I am aware of the dangers of allowing the arc of my words to sweep too broadly, for there are always exceptions, and it is certainly not my intention to trivialise the immediacy, or the devastation, caused by abject material poverty, but I have seen first-hand around the world that wealth of spirit is more often than not the heirloom of impoverished communities. Each day that I walk the dusty roads of Swaziland, I meet millionaires clothed as the humble poor.

Often at the bedside of a dying patient, Matron Zwane will ask me to sing. In those moments there is an intimacy that transcends barriers of language and ethnicity, and so it is that in Swaziland I have become known as the 'singing doctor'.

The choir we have formed in Siteki has attracted many young people. They sing in the most rural and remote communities of the Lubombo region. And they have a charter, to use music as a tool for empowerment and healing. They sing at meetings of the Community Committee, at the opening of houses and vegetable gardens established by our team, and for many patients and families who are afflicted by AIDS and extreme poverty.

I never cease to be amazed when the members of the choir hold hands outside a little mud hut and sing their traditional Swazi songs to a sick or dying person inside, or when they sit at the bedside of someone who has been paralysed by the neurological complications of AIDS— lifting the roof with their extraordinary harmonies.

In those moments, presence is more than physical. There is an invisible exchange that occurs in the spaces between each of us. When we allow the barriers to fall away, for even the most fleeting moment, and to create a genuine intimacy between ourselves and another human being, presence becomes an art form, it becomes an instrument of empowerment.

As I go out into communities this morning, to visit those living with AIDS, malnutrition, and extreme poverty, my wish is to be fully and vibrantly present—to create a space in which I am receptive to the invitation of woundedness, another's and my own.

Perhaps it is from such a space that true healing can begin.

From Siteki with love,

Maithri

It's how we roll

I have a car in Siteki that I use during the months of the year that I am in Swaziland, and when I'm back in Australia my car is used by our team or by volunteers. Matron refers to it jokingly as our 'Swazi car', honouring its extraordinary resilience; and this month in particular it has been through a lot. I'm sure whoever built it had no idea that it would one day be navigating the most remote areas of the Lubombo Mountains—buffeting through untamed fields of tall grass, and screeching along gravel roads and pathways made almost entirely from giant, jagged-edged rocks. In four weeks, I have had nine flat tyres, my spark plugs have exploded once, the battery has died twice, and the fuel tank was ruptured on a very large, knife-edged rock.

That kind of automotive abuse is an unfortunate peril of our work. The poorest people tend to live in the most difficult to access areas. And yet, unlike the frustration that might happen in Australia when faced with a broken-down vehicle, Swaziland has taught me not to take it at all too seriously. We take it as a moment to talk about what's been happening in the day. Matron will start singing, and the younger members of our team will start making jokes about how much we had planned to get done that day. Children from the community will often come down and investigate what all the commotion is about, and we will play games and dance with them.

In Swaziland, little things are honoured—little spaces between moments that can be filled with laughter, music, and human connection. So when the tyre goes flat on the Lubombo Plateau and we look in the trunk to find the spare is also flat and someone has stolen the pump, we do not despair; we simply gather together a ragtag band and walk into the grassy communities in search of a bicycle pump or a working mobile phone, laughing all the way.

The other day, our youngest team member Thando was driving my car through Siteki when a cow suddenly and without warning ran directly into the passenger side. Cows are among the most dangerous things on Swazi roads, and have no respect for traffic rules and regulations. Many people have died, especially at night, from collisions with stealthy cows standing virtually unseen in the middle of an unlit road. On this occasion the cow survived, but my car was in a critical condition.

Thando managed to drive it back to the farm where I was staying. I came out to watch as my vehicle rattled and squeaked down the path with lights hanging by wires and the entire passenger side crumpled in like an accordion.

Finally, Thando got out of the car, almost in tears, and said, 'I'm so sorry, *Dokotela*, it was a cow.'

I put my arm around him and replied, 'It's okay, Thando; it's a Swazi car.'

In Swaziland, life goes on.

From Siteki with love,

Maithri

Hlane

We placed them in a semi-circle: four old drums used for carrying water—two red and two yellow, with their mouths worn and their bodies sun-damaged and dusty, just like most of the possessions owned by young families in the rural village of Hlane.

My heart raced in my chest as I sat down on the yellow drum, my elected seat for the moment I had been dreading.

The night before, I had been leading the choir in rehearsal, when Beki and Cyprian, two of our young male team members, came to me with urgency in their voices.

'*Dokotela*, we need to speak to you. It is important.'

They walked me silently into our little, brown office, and I found Matron already sitting, waiting for me, on the long pew from the church that we had been using as a seat.

'What's happened, Matron?' I asked.

Slowly and quietly, Matron began. She spoke of a young family in the remote community of Hlane whom our team had been visiting for some time. Hlane is famous in Swaziland, not for its human inhabitants, but for its animals. It is home to one of Swaziland's most visited national reserves which boasts the famous 'big five'—lion, leopard, water buffalo, elephant, and white rhino.

The family we had been seeing lived outside the national park. They were incredibly poor and had very little access to basics like food and water. They comprised of a mother, father, and three children, the youngest was just over six months old.

On a recent visit to the homestead we had noticed that the children and mother were coughing, which raised immediate concerns: perhaps the father's virulent strain of tuberculosis had spread. Beki and Cyprian had advised the family that they should come to the hospital and be tested. The team gave the family bus fares and then informed the paediatrician, Dr Joyce Mareverwa from Zimbabwe, whom I had worked with professionally for many years.

The next day the family arrived. The mother carried her infant strapped tightly to her back with a piece of cloth, as is the tradition in Swaziland. After her initial assessment, Joyce thought it wise to admit the mother and her baby for further tests, but she felt the other two children, the two boys aged nine and eleven, were healthy enough to go home.

The two children were given bus fares for their return trip, which they had made independently many times before, and so they were sent on their way.

Matron stopped in the middle of telling the story. It was dark and the lights in the office barely lit up her face. The young men, Beki and Cyprian, sat beside her in silence, their eyes wide.

'What's happened, Matron? Is it the diagnosis? Was it positive?'

'No, *Dokotela*,' she continued. 'Just as the boys had got down from the bus there was a truck coming in the opposite direction. It was going too fast. The eleven-year-old managed to get out of the way, but the nine-year-old was struck.'

'Matron, is he ok?' I asked earnestly.

Matron, Beki, and Cyprian looked down at the floor.

'Matron?'

'He was killed, *Dokotela*,' she said softly.

'No,' was all I could say as I tried to process what I had just been told.

'*Make* does not know what has happened to her son, *Dokotela*,' Beki continued, his voice trembling. 'She has been admitted to the ward.' He paused. 'What do you want us to do, *Dokotela*?'

They looked at me expectantly.

'Matron, what do we do?' I asked.

Matron looked at the three of us and said, 'We don't do anything now.' She took a deep breath. 'To tell *Make* tonight, in the coldness of a hospital ward, when she is alone, would be wrong. We must take her back to Hlane in the morning, and then, with the women in the community, we must sit her down, *Dokotela*, and tell her in a place where she will feel supported.'

'Of course. Thank you, Matron,' I replied.

The drive to Hlane the next morning was excruciating. We had split up into two cars, carrying Matron, Cyprian,

Beki, John, who was an Australian volunteer, *Make* and her baby, and a female nurse from the Hlane Clinic. *Make* sat with her child in the back of the car that I was in; she was completely unaware of what had happened and what the rest of us were struggling with and would soon have to reveal to her.

The sun was rising as we drove, and we passed impalas and large antelopes, known as inyala, feeding on nearby bushes. Occasionally they would dart across our path in the misty morning light.

We picked up a few family members on the way who knew what had happened and wanted to be present when *Make* and *Babe*, mother and father, were told. Both cars were soon full.

Finally we arrived at the homestead.

Babe was taken by the men behind his hut where they told him the news. He fell to his knees, placed his hands over his eyes, and wept.

Matron gestured to me that it was time to tell *Make*.

We were all worried about what *Make* might do when she heard the news. The nurse from the clinic who knew her well was ready to take the baby from her and allow her to scream or shout or do whatever she needed to do. We wanted to create a safe space for her to grieve.

We gathered four water containers together on the dry earth outside her hut. Matron sat next to *Make*, with the clinic nurse on the opposite side. I was given the container on the end.

Make was wearing her best black-and-white dress. Swazis show respect to health care workers by wearing their best clothes to the hospital. It has always amazed me. They may often own so little, but there will be something that they will keep just to wear to 'important places' like the hospital.

Make held her baby in her arms and began to feed it with a teaspoon.

Matron stood up from her seat and began to speak. Her voice was resonant and deep, as she described, in siSwati, what had happened.

My eyes were fixed on *Make* who was listening intently while continuing to feed her baby.

'And then, after they stepped from the bus, there was a truck that was going too fast,' Matron said. And as she continued, *Make* looked up for a moment, at the sky. 'We are so sorry but he was killed.'

Make said nothing, the spoon in her hand falling to the ground. She took one long deep breath and looked down at the baby in her arms. Then after a few long, empty moments she picked up the spoon and cleaned it with a cloth. Slowly, she dipped it once again into the food and placed it back into her baby's mouth as large teardrops welled in her eyes.

For a few minutes no one moved. No one said a word. She just kept feeding her baby, carefully, patiently, one mouthful at a time, as she cried in almost complete silence.

For how long, I am not certain, but for some time we sat next to her on our makeshift seats as the morning sun took its place in the sky.

From Siteki with love,

Maithri

Vula Bevalile

I spent yesterday with Matron Anna Zwane. For many decades, she has worked as a senior nurse in the rural areas of sub-Saharan Africa.

Long before sustainability and local empowerment became the new paradigm of international development, Matron Zwane was a living instrument of emancipation for her people.

From Kenya to Malawi, KwaZulu Natal to her home in Swaziland, she has lived a life of potency and influence, devoting her life to the service of those who are suffering in remote communities.

Her short stature is deceptive. Matron Zwane is the most powerful person I know.

Yesterday, as we spoke about a family of orphans in the hills of Mambane, Matron said to me, 'Yes, those children need food, but I know that there is a family nearby that grows jugo beans and another family that has had a large harvest of maize this year. Let us call upon them to see if they can help these children before we seek assistance elsewhere.'

That is the kind of advice we receive from her every day of the year. I've lost count of the number of times I have wanted to go ahead with a project only to be pulled back by Matron.

I'm now familiar with the process: we will both see a problem; I will come up with what I think is a perfectly sensible solution; she will patiently hear me out, becoming very still; and then, after a pause, she will raise her finger and measuredly say, 'You see ...' carefully and patiently explaining to me why my 'solution' is completely inappropriate.

In her explanations, Matron often uses the word 'culturally', which she emphasises as 'cultur-a-lly'.

'No, I understand it sounds good to you, *Dokotela*, but "cultur-a-lly" that just would not work. Let me show you the Swazi way.'

Matron is my teacher. I am constantly learning from her.

One day, a few years ago, Matron Anna and I were driving behind a dusty bus on the road that runs from Siteki to Lonhlupheko. Swazi buses are famous for the pithy and often unintentionally amusing sayings that they have written on their sides. Sayings like, 'The Lord is my shepherd for hire'.

This particular bus had two words written in siSwati underneath the rear window: '*Vula Bevalile*'.

'What does that mean?' I asked.

'It means, when you come to a door that's closed, you need to open it anyway. It may be bolted; it may be locked; that does not matter; open it! Just open it!'

I thought for a moment and then replied, 'I pity the door that stands in the way of you, Anna Zwane.'

She chuckled—her shoulders rocking back and forth, her warmth filling the confines of my dusty, shuddering car.

'So, *Vula*,' she smiled, her eyes sparkling, 'that will be your Swazi name. It will help you in your work.'

'I'm honoured, Matron, that is a beautiful name.' I was trying to absorb the moment while still keeping an eye on the road. I spoke the name out loud to myself, feeling the words on my tongue.

'*Vu-la Beva-li-le*. Open the closed door! What a cool nickname, Matron.'

She paused. Her tone was gentle but serious.

'It is not just a name, my son. It's a command!'

From Siteki with love,

Maithri

Andile's story

In the quiet heart of rural Swaziland, there are communities, like Sitsatsaweni, where the wind and amber grass pursue their romance undisturbed by the world, and donkeys daydream on the dusty roads.

My friend Andile was born in Sitsatsaweni. From the day of his birth, the cold shadow of adversity has followed him, but I have never once heard him complain.

Andile was born with spina bifida, a condition where the embryonic neural tube doesn't fully close, leading to openings in the vertebrae overlying the spinal cord. From a very early age, his legs have been essentially paralysed.

But despite his misfortune, Andile looks at the world with great tolerance and understanding. His voice is tender like laughter, his smile forever gentle, kind, and forgiving.

Andile spent the first eleven years of his life held captive within the walls of a dimly lit mud hut in Sitsatsaweni. It was there that he would crawl on his hands, dragging his lifeless legs behind him. For eleven years, the only time he ever left the hut was to attend hospital for chronic infections in his legs.

One day, it was just before his twelfth birthday, Andile was bathing. He looked down at his feet and saw a stream of yellow pus oozing from his legs. When he washed away the ooze, he found that the bones of his feet had pierced the skin.

He was rushed to hospital where he was told that the infection was so severe that they would have to amputate both his legs.

His life was saved, but Andile was devastated.

Into Andile's life there would come an angel. Her name was Kathleen, and she was a nurse from New York. Kathleen's love for the people of Swaziland was fierce and unwavering. She never sought glory or acclaim, never put herself above her patients. She wanted only to sit with others, to help ease their pain, holding their hands through it all.

Kathleen was welcomed by Andile's family. She helped arrange for Andile to receive a wheelchair and for him to go to school. For a time, it seemed that things were finally improving for him. He was sent to a boarding school for students with special needs and disabilities in one of the biggest towns in Swaziland. For four years, he flourished there and grew in strength and spirit with the support and love from his family and his friends like Kathleen.

Then it happened that a new boarding master came to the school. He was the antithesis of everything Andile had become. The boarding master was cruel and unkind, and he became deeply jealous of the support that Andile received from Kathleen.

'You know you're not deserving of this,' he would say, pointing to Andile's mobile phone. 'Give it to me!' At every possible juncture he would find an opportunity to tell Andile that he was unworthy.

One day, things erupted. Without provocation, the boarding master told Andile, 'You are useless: you are sixteen and can't read or write properly. The only reason you're here is because of the *umlungu*, the white lady. There is no future for you.'

In his room that evening, Andile sank into his wheelchair, his eyes red with tears. He decided that if his boarding master believed that his life had no meaning, then it must be true, and therefore there was no reason to go on.

He went to the trunk in which he kept his belongings and found a length of rope. Knowing that it would be too short to hang himself with, he took his belt and tied the end to it. Placing the hybrid rope in a bag and leaving his wheelchair behind, he started to crawl on his hands and the stumps of his feet into the forest next to the boarding school.

As the evening shadows fell, Andile went deeper into the forest. By that time there were people out searching for him, and every now and then he glimpsed the long, yellow beam of a flashlight or heard the muffled cries of the motley search party of friends and whoever they could find to help.

It was then that he came to a strong, old tree which he knew was capable of holding his weight.

Sitting under the arms of that tree, he said a prayer.

'I have read in the Bible that people who commit suicide go to hell. But if you can see me, if you can see my life, then you will know that any hell which you send me to will be better than this place. So forgive me for what I am about to do and watch over the ones I love.'

With those words, he found a strong branch and readied himself.

He put his hand into the bag to pull out the rope, wanting it all to be over quickly.

To his surprise, the rope was gone.

For a moment he couldn't breathe, could not understand what had happened. He looked everywhere, but there was no sign of the rope that he was so certain he had carried with him.

As he continued to look around him, quietness fell over the forest. His heart calmed, and for a moment it felt as if he was in Sitsatsaweni again; it was as if the voice deep inside him, the voice that had carried him so far through such difficult times, had returned and could not be completely silenced. His loneliness began to ease, and he started back to school.

When I look at the trajectory Andile's life has taken since that fateful evening, I am amazed at the manifold ways in which his humility and indomitable spirit have touched the lives of all those around him. Andile has now begun singing in the choir that we set up, and while he adores his involvement as a singer, he is also able to share his vision of hope with a diversity of groups around Swaziland and beyond.

From Siteki with love,

Maithri

Bugs

I have always been a fan of the television series 'Man vs Wild'. In it, a man who is aptly named 'Bear' is literally dropped into the wilderness with only a Swiss army knife and the shirt on his back. Granted, I think he is a former member of the SAS, a special air service unit of the British army, but through will power, determination, and a steady diet of insects, seeds, and various other 'natural delicacies' he has to not only survive but find a way out of the most rugged and inhospitable terrain on the planet.

I am considering making my own television show. I will call it 'Maithri vs Bugs'.

It will consist of Maithri being dropped in Swaziland, and then being killed by bugs. I know that might not sound like a ratings winner, but it would be pretty close to the truth.

For the past two weeks, the prehistoric, black denizen of my room, whom I have named 'Dude', seems to have acquired wings, and at various hours of the night starts flying around my room like Wesley Snipes …

And as Wesley himself once admonished, 'Always bet on black!'

Last night, as a consequence of the rains, a different flying insect, the size of a bat, which I'm sure co-starred with Dude in the last Jurassic Park movie, came into our house and landed on our kitchen ceiling. I took a long pole and tried to gently nudge it back into the garden. I succeeded only in causing 'Batman' to fly down to eye level, where, for a few seconds, he stared at me, with his beady little eyes, as if sizing me up, and then quite literally started chasing me around the house. In the end I conceded defeat and ran out the front door into the safety of the pouring rain.

Ah well. As my friend, Bear, might say, 'Better wet than dead!'

From Siteki with love,

Maithri

INNOCENCE

Children, in their innocence, their resilience, and their love, have so much to teach those of us who have turned into 'serious adults', doctors included.

If ever a book existed called 'The Tao of Ice Cream', the first page would read, 'Live now. Live well. Taste the moment.'

Nowhere are the lessons we can learn from our children more readily apparent than here in this little mountain country where orphaned children make up ten percent of the population.

Since my first trip to Swaziland, visiting the Hlane National Park has been how we regularly spend our weekends. It feels like we have taken a thousand kids to Hlane—sometimes in wheelchairs, or covered in burns or sores or Kaposi's sarcoma, or sometimes with an intravenous line still in their hands, but always with dreams of lions and elephants in their heads.

On a recent trip to the national park, with some of the children from the paediatric ward, I met Nelsiwe. Nelsiwe is a six-year-old girl with skin the smoothness of porcelain and wide brown eyes that would make Bambi squirm with envy.

Of all the children I have taken there, Nelsiwe has by far been the quietest. Even with all my clowning around and silliness, it was hard to make a soft smile break upon the shores of her beautiful face.

Nelsiwe was born to a very poor homestead, even by Swazi standards. Her mother was infected with AIDS and died shortly after giving birth to Nelsiwe. In her family, only her grandparents and her father remained.

At the age of five, Nelsiwe was admitted to hospital and diagnosed with pelvic trauma, most likely as a secondary condition of sexual abuse.

At the age of six, she was readmitted with genital warts. It was at that time that steps were taken to remove her from her homestead, and she has been in hospital ever since.

When I first met Nelsiwe, the sadness which a child should never have to endure was written all over her face, etched into her ways of being and her behaviour.

I have often asked myself, 'How could anyone hurt something so tender, so beautiful, so wholly innocent? And why does child abuse often become more common in communities where people are impoverished and destitute?'

I still don't have the answers to those questions, not with any certainty, but a friend, who I respect very much, once suggested that sexual abuse has less to do with the sexual act than it does with the dynamics of power and disempowerment.

After a few hours of driving and dancing, I asked Nelsiwe what her favourite animal was.

'Impala,' she said softly. I smiled. Impalas are among the gentlest animals I have seen. They are always listening to the wind, alert to the slightest sound that might herald the approach of danger.

Nelsiwe told me that they look very kind, like goats, and she asked if she could take one home to the hospital.

By day's end, after a meal of pizza and ice cream, her smiles came much easier. And as I walked her back to the paediatric ward, she offered me her tiny hand in a wordless gesture of trust.

I wanted to tell her how beautiful she was, how priceless, how nothing that she had been through could tarnish the beauty within her. But as I saw her face beaming with confidence, and her head held high, words seemed unnecessary.

I held her soft hand in mine and walked with her back to the ward.

From Siteki with love,

Maithri

DIFFERENCES

Recently I was in the community of Ngcina, a place where the green aloe constellates like stars beside the red dust road. As we drove there, I was reminded of some of the wonderful people I work with. In the back seat of our truck were two Swazi nurses, *Make* Maposa and Matron Zwane, who both display enormous dignity and persistent gentleness in the face of despair. They are a great source of inspiration to all those fortunate enough to be in their presence. And in the driver's seat was my wonderful friend and teammate Kathleen, who is with us again from New York, not only as a nurse, but to share her gift of true compassion.

Often when I look at the people who travel in our truck, I am truly grateful for what they bring with them. As well as our equipment and medical supplies, our truck is full of love. Love is the most potent tool we have, and the most necessary.

We had already seen many people in need of care—patients with end-stage HIV, and sick, orphaned children—when we came upon a little one-bedroom home made of cement.

Lying on a mattress inside that home was a man covered in a blanket.

'*Sanibonani*,' he greeted us, softly.

Clearly, he was suffering. I asked if I could examine him, and drew back the blanket. From thigh to toe, his legs were covered in long, cavernous ulcers—ulcers that had eaten through skin, soft tissue, and even muscle.

On close inspection it was clear that the ulcers were infected with the almost fluorescent yellow-green exudate that is characteristic of infection from a bacterium known as *Pseudomonas aeruginosa*. Thick, pungent pus poured like honey from his wounds. His bed was awash with oozing sickness.

We lifted one leg and found that his heels were covered in cavitating lesions that were eating into his ankle joints. Having no dressings to put on his wounds, he had used old newspaper, which had now adhered to his legs.

He had been languishing in the final stages of HIV, and

had not walked in many months because of nerve damage caused by the virus.

I cannot imagine what it is like to go to sleep at night with a bed covered in wet, infected pus, to be unable to get up and clean yourself, to endure the pain of knowing that every day the infection is moving further up your body.

We cleaned his wounds, dressed them as well as we could, then gave him some medications and organised for him to come to the hospital for immediate surgical debridement and intravenous antibiotics.

As I looked around the walls of his cement home I saw a photo positioned directly above the foot of his bed.

'Who is that?' I asked.

'My daughter, Zandile, *Dokotela*,' he responded.

'She is beautiful,' I said with a smile.

'Yes, I love her,' he whispered. 'I keep it there because when I see her face it makes the pain go away for a moment.'

When we hear about Africa or the developing world, we hear of diseases and poverty of such unimaginable intensity and perplexity that it almost seems unreal.

Perhaps by way of defence we have created for ourselves the idea of a 'third world', a construct that becomes a home for all the uncomfortable realities of human existence with which we would rather not engage. By labelling something as a 'third world' or as a 'developing world' we alienate ourselves from it. And yet the inhabitants of those worlds remain just as tender and salient as those who live in our world.

There, in Ngcina, in a cement house, resides a person who is not just another 'third world' victim of HIV. In that house is a man, a human being just like us. And that man loves his children, just as we love ours. And in the height of his sorrow he looks upon the face of his daughter and finds a breath of hope and courage.

The deeper my work in Swaziland takes me into the unknown, into the ignored, the more I realise that we are not as different as we often lead ourselves to believe.

From Siteki with love,

Maithri

Gogo Maziya

Gogo Maziya is my friend. Her frail, aging body reminds me of the fever trees that grow by the side of the road in many parts of the Lubombo area—slender and delicate, and yet strangely luminous and unmistakeably alive.

Known for her gentle determination and wide unforced smile, she has lived her seventy-four years in the red dust hills of Makhewu.

Gogo Maziya has raised five of her own children. All of them eventually contracted HIV/AIDS, and one by one, *Gogo* Maziya watched them suffer and die. As each one passed away, she took in their children, her newly orphaned grandchildren, into her little cement home with only two rooms.

At the last count, there were seventeen children staying with *Gogo* Maziya. Two more children from another deceased relative were also on the way.

One day, while out walking with another dear friend, *Make* Nomsa Bhembe, we stopped at *Gogo* Maziya's house and saw her many grandchildren playing barefoot outside. We thought we would take a moment to say hello to *Gogo* Maziya, and maybe play a game with the children.

As I walked into her house, the faint scent of urine hung in the air—one of the hard realities of having so many children sleeping together in one room.

A little baby was fast asleep in the corner, and *Gogo* Maziya was standing by a dusty, yellow wall, her whole attention focused on something she was holding in her hand.

'What's that?' I asked, greeting her with a smile. She jumped, startled by our presence.

After welcoming us with a fond embrace, *Gogo* Maziya answered, 'Rat poison.'

'*Gogo*, are the rats bothering you?' I asked, Nomsa translating for me.

'No, the rats are okay. This is for me!' she laughed.

'For you?' *Make* Nomsa Bhembe and I were deeply concerned.

'I would not take it. Don't worry. But it is hard sometimes when all your children have died, when every day you have to look after seventeen babies. I feel like there is no point sometimes.'

'What stops you taking the poison, *Gogo*?' Nomsa asked.

'The children. I hear them playing outside. I know they need me. I am all they have in this world.'

'So this is a decision you made a long time ago, *Gogo*, to never take this rat poison?'

'No,' she continued in siSwati, shaking her head, 'it is a decision I make every day. Every day I think about it. I know exactly where the poison sits on the shelf. But every day I hear those children playing. So I say to myself, "Not today!"'

From Siteki with love,

Maithri

BUSISWA

If mischief had a human incarnation, it would be called Busiswa. Busiswa is a six-year-old boy who lives in the rural community of Ngcina, which is located at the base of the Lubombo Mountains. As vigilantly as his loving *Gogo* tries to keep him clean and tidy, he seems perpetually covered in a thick layer of red dust, and his one little, purple sweater is dotted with ragged holes from his many close encounters with chickens and thorn bushes.

Busiswa has AIDS, and his child's life has been plagued by periods of serious illness and hospitalisation. Because of the way AIDS renders the immune system weak and susceptible to opportunistic infections, Busiswa has already had tuberculosis and multiple brain and nervous system infections. It was complications from encephalitis and meningitis that left him with his now characteristic 'lazy eye'.

I would imagine that a still-life image of Busiswa, with his bloated stomach, spindly limbs, and head so sparsely covered with brittle hair, would be a sobering and solemn sight. However, in reality there is almost nothing 'still' about Busiswa. He is alive—vibrantly and mischievously alive!

One of Busiswa's favourite games has come to be affectionately known as 'Throw the cat on the Doctor'. It begins with a doctor, namely me, walking through the dry homestead where Busiswa lives with his loving *Gogo* and five siblings. Busiswa secretly captures the near-skeletal, playful cat that wanders daily through his homestead. The cat seems to have a special affection for Busiswa, submitting to his handling without protest. With the cat in his arms, Busiswa crouches behind a bush or the side of his hut like a lion waiting for its prey.

The moment I walk by, the poor feline is hurled suddenly towards me. Busiswa has the timing and precision of a marksman. I often wonder whether it is the furious frenzy of claw and fur, as gangly legs reach desperately for my shirt, that brings him such joy, or simply my reaction to the events as they unfold hilariously before him. No matter how many times it happens, I always seem to be caught off guard, running frantically in a strange dance trying to calm the poor animal while also trying to regain my own composure and to protect myself.

Then from behind his hiding place I hear a familiar murmur—the sound of Busiswa's sly giggle. After a few moments it turns into rollicking laughter, as his body shakes back and forth. Almost inevitably he falls to the floor, kicking his legs about from the force of extreme delight, with tears of joy streaming down his cheeks. As we watch on, his *gogo*, the other children, and I are somehow transported into the joy of his world. A sudden wave of sweet laughter washes over everyone in that dry, desolate homestead. It is a sound as comforting as rain.

From Siteki with love

Maithri

* * *

Today, one day after I returned to Australia, I heard the news that little Busiswa had collapsed. It seems that the ARVs, the anti-retroviral medications for his AIDS, had overwhelmed his kidneys, and he had gone into sudden kidney failure.

His *gogo* had rushed him to hospital and sat by his bedside holding his hand for almost twenty-four hours. Then, just after two o'clock this morning, Busiswa died.

Gogo doesn't have money for a coffin or clothes to bury him in. Matron and the team are with her, and will help her through this painful and delicate time. For the moment, we are all in a state of shock. All I can think about is that mischievous laughter; it plays over and over in my mind like the sweet fragment of a song.

How will the world survive without it?

Maithri

It's not easy being green

As a teenager I once watched a documentary about phobias. It contained profiles on a range of people with intense fears—everything from a fear of heights to a fear of clowns. And the complementary narration really enforced just how debilitating those phobias could be.

The story of one particular woman stayed in my mind. She was afraid of frogs.

A re-enactment showed her sitting down one morning at her kitchen table to open her mail when she noticed that one of the letters she had received had a stamp with a little green frog on it. With a blood-curdling scream she threw the letters to the farthest corner of the room and jumped onto her kitchen table in a state of pure hysteria.

At the time I thought it was the funniest thing I had ever seen.

Since then I have learnt that perhaps her fears were not totally unfounded.

Over the years, my relationship with frogs, or any amphibians for that matter, has been largely unremarkable. I leave them alone and they offer me the same courtesy. We don't get in each other's way.

Two nights ago, however, I awoke at three in the morning, needing to visit the bathroom. As I sat, half asleep on the toilet, I noticed something on the wall. It was a small, spectacularly coloured frog—emerald green with blood red legs.

I was startled by its beauty and couldn't wait to grab my camera to take a photo. But before I had time to stand and wash my hands, the little creature jumped, straight up, about two or three metres, and landed on the ceiling.

'Bravo!' I said. 'What talent!'

Then he seemed to be readying himself for another death-defying leap. I watched, mesmerised, as his little eyes shone like black diamonds, and he arched his body up and down from the ceiling. Then, with a flash, he leapt again.

My eyes scanned the floor and the walls, but I couldn't see him anywhere. Then, to my surprise, as I turned my head I saw him. He was sitting on my right shoulder, looking directly at me.

Immediately my mind flew back to the 'frog lady' in that documentary I had seen all those years ago. Did she know something I didn't? Was the little, slimy guy, sitting on my shoulder, just centimetres away from my nose, friend or foe?

Unfortunately, at that moment I also remembered that it is the brightly coloured frogs that tended to be the most poisonous. The toxins that they secrete through their skin act as an effective defence against predators, but that also meant that touching some of the more poisonous species could cause skin irritation, hallucinations, or even death.

Not wanting to take any chances, I did what most sane people would do at three in the morning when a potentially dangerous frog has just jumped onto their shoulder. I decided to talk him down.

'Hi.'

Frog: Silence.

'How are you?'

Frog: Silence again.

'So what brings you to Swaziland?'

Frog: Silence.

'You're not very talkative are you?'

Frog: Silence.

'So, are you poisonous?'

Frog: More Silence.

'Please don't hurt me.'

Frog: Silence.

'Are you going to jump on my face?'

Frog: Long awkward silence.

'Ummm, no offence, but shouldn't you be in the Amazon?'

With those words, my silent visitor made a guttural noise as if to say, 'That's not funny, dude,' and catapulted to another wall before beginning to hurl himself at light speed from wall to floor to ceiling, like some kind of insane green ninja.

As I sat helpless in the midst of the crazy, amphibian acrobatics being displayed all around me, trying to protect my face from what I had now surmised could indeed be potentially lethal Amazonian frog venom, I vowed never again to laugh at anyone's fears, especially 'frog lady' and her stamps.

From Siteki with love,

Maithri

BLISTERED FEET

Take the deepest shade of green, texture it with ochre dust, add the infinite curves of a mountain range, and layer it with fields of wild, yellow grass. Then people it with gentleness and little smiles breaking on the shores of unimaginable pain, and you will glimpse the Lubombo I know.

One Sunday afternoon after visiting some patients in the communities surrounding the hospital, I decided to take a leisurely drive along the dirt road that extends from Maphungwane to Big Bend. The road is long, and littered with jagged rocks and pot holes, but it affords stunning panoramic views of Swaziland's Lubombo Mountains when descending from Maphungwane to the plains below.

I had not driven more than a kilometre when I noticed an older Swazi woman walking the same road. She had a ten kilo bag of maize meal on her head, and neatly wrapped under her arm was what seemed to be a little blanket.

Opening my window I asked in my awkward siSwati, '*Make*, can I give you a lift?'

Her time-sculpted face was etched in hues of dignity. Without a word she removed the maize meal from her head, put it in the trunk of my car, and with the smallest of smiles we recommenced our journey.

She was a woman of few words. I explained that I was a doctor, and that I came each year to work with the people. She told me that her home was just a 'little way'.

We drove down the steep gravel road, past huts of mud and thatch, some in disrepair from recent storms. Barefoot toddlers with muddy legs and wild smiles waved and blew kisses from the side of the road as we passed.

After driving for fifteen minutes I asked, 'Is it close, *Make*?'

'*Hamba embile*,' she whispered, urging me to keep going.

So we did. Seemingly suicidal goats appeared in front of us, as they weaved in and out of mothers and children carrying large containers of freshly collected water on their heads for their evening ablutions.

As the sun set around us, we came to a sugar plantation. I decided that this must be the place where *Make* stayed.

I nodded, 'Here?'

'*Hamba embile*,' came the quiet reply once again. So we continued on, driving through acres of towering green sugar cane.

After another half an hour we came to a muddy river. The signage beside it was ominous, 'Beware, hippos and crocodiles.'

I wondered how anyone could walk that far, especially with a ten kilo bag of maize on their head. '*Make*, surely you do not walk this whole way?' I asked incredulously. 'Is there a bus or Kombi that runs here?'

'No bus. No Kombi.'

'How long does this walk take you?'

She explained that she was going to her workplace in Big Bend, having left from her home in Maphungwane. 'I leave at two in the afternoon and arrive in Big Bend at seven-thirty at night.'

That's five hours and thirty minutes, I calculated in astonishment.

As the first long shadows of night began to fall, we arrived at a line of little homes on the outskirts of another sugar plantation. We were in Big Bend, the place where one of *Make's* daughters also worked. Every weekend, *Make* would return to Maphungwane to visit the many grandchildren under her care and ensure they had enough money for food, schooling, and living expenses the following week. As we drove the final few metres into the sugar plantation, *Make* told me the rest of her story.

'Last night, I was here in Big Bend grinding leaves to sell at market. Suddenly, my eldest daughter, who stays next door to me, cried out for help. She was in labour and delivered a tiny baby girl. But the baby was struggling to breathe.

'We knew we had to get the child to hospital, but there was no bus, and I had no money.

'It was dark and cold. We walked to a neighbour's house and borrowed a baby's blanket so that we could keep our new infant warm.

'My daughter held the baby to her breast as we began to walk. With every step the little child grew more and more breathless.

'Then, when we were just beyond the sugar plantation, the little one stopped breathing.

'My daughter cradled her baby's lifeless body in her arms for five-and-a-half hours as we walked up the hillside to our home in Maphungwane. She kissed her and spoke to her as if she were alive.

'When we reached our homestead this morning, we buried the child in the fields of long grass next to my home.'

I stopped the car, not knowing what to say.

The 'concerned doctor' in me wanted to do something to help. Holding her hand I said, 'Why were you walking back to work today? It is obvious that you are grieving. You should be at home with your family, not walking another five-and-a-half hours to work. Can I please drive you back to your homestead so you can be with your daughter?'

A quiet dignity fell over her face. She smiled at me and whispered.

'*Dokotela*, I am not going to work.

'I am going to return the blanket that we borrowed last night.'

From Siteki with love,

Maithri

Araliya

I was born in Sri Lanka—a place where the jungle daily marries the tropical sea, and smiles remain the great social currency. In spite of her blood-stained past, the Sri Lanka I know is sumptuously alive with flavour, rhythm, and fragrance. Her sacred flower is the Araliya, or temple flower, known in English as the Frangipani. Simple white petals cascading from a yellow heart are the icons of purity and are offered as a religious or spiritual sacrifice in many diverse traditions. The very scent of Araliya is enough to conjure images of the great metaphysical mysteries of life. Working as I do now in Australia and Swaziland, I rarely see the Araliya anymore. But a few days ago in the most unexpected of places—a poor rural homestead in Manhlege, Swaziland—she was everywhere.

As we approached the rudimentary mud-and-stick home, I noticed two great Araliya trees in vibrant bloom. Thembi, one of our beautiful and brilliantly innovative Swazi project coordinators, had already told me about the old man who lived there.

'His name is Manyosi Maziya, and the first time I met him he asked me to marry him, Doc!' She laughed.

'Well, Thembi, it's clear that the man has both taste and intelligence,' I replied, smiling.

'*Sanibonani Ekhaya,*' Thembi called into the mud hut, asking if anyone was home.

Slowly, from the darkness of the interior, an old man appeared. He was quite literally bent in two, holding a walking stick. His clothes were torn and covered in several thick layers of dirt. His hair was dishevelled, his face muddy.

When Thembi explained why we had come, he immediately grabbed my hand and pulled me awkwardly into the hut. He wanted to give me a guided tour.

Inside there were two little rooms. The deep-brown mud was broken in places allowing drifting beams of light to gently wash over the dirty bed and pots and pans that comprised all of his belongings.

I noticed that the second room was padlocked.

'What do you keep in there, Mkhulu?' I asked, Thembi translating.

'My box of treasures,' he answered.

I was intrigued.

As we stepped towards the flimsy wooden door, Mkhulu grew visibly more excited. We lingered there for a few moments as he fumbled with the key, which he drew from his dirty, ragged pants pocket. As we entered the darkness, I faintly saw a wooden box sitting in a corner. It was quite large, about knee height, and as I looked closer I could see that it was lovingly decorated with a faded, blue sheet and ribbons made from strips of coloured cloth. Slowly he opened the lid. Mkhulu could not afford a second padlock, but he had found a device almost as effective to guard his precious box. I saw an initial compartment designed to distract thieves into believing the box contained nothing more than a few old plastic bags. Mkhulu showed me how the compartment was readily removable, revealing the treasures that lay beneath.

He looked at me and grinned like a toothless schoolboy. Then, taking my hand in his, he reached down into the box and began pulling out other plastic bags, filled with items. He clutched each one to his chest, before opening them gently and handing the contents to me.

Inside the bags were clothes—brand new clothes—some for men and others for women and children. There were dresses and floral hats.

'Where did you get these from, Mkhulu?' Thembi asked.

Mkhulu Maziya explained that he had purchased them with money he received each month from the government's 'elderly grant'.

'And they are all for you?' I asked with a smile, looking at the beautiful blue dress inside the bag I had just opened.

He chuckled, 'No, these are not for me. They are for the poor.'

'When I see a poor person walking past my home, I reach into my box and give them a gift.

'It all started one day when I was walking to Big Bend: I saw a man who had no clothes. I heard a voice inside me say, "Take off your jacket and give it to him." I did. Then I came home and took all the money I had, and bought clothes for the poor. Now, every month, when I receive my pension, I take just enough to eat, and with the rest I buy these clothes.'

'But what about you, Mkhulu?' I asked, looking at his own dirty, ripped clothes, and at his house of mud that was clearly falling apart around him, 'Why don't you buy something for yourself?'

Thembi translated, 'He says he has no need for earthly things, Doc.'

'Here,' he gestured to me and then to a shiny red hat. 'Take it, it's yours,' he said smiling.

As his eyes twinkled in the darkness, I noticed something that I had not been aware of when I entered his home made of mud and sticks—the quiet fragrance of temple flowers.

From Siteki with love,

Maithri

THE DANCE

When I first met *Gogo* Ndzimandze, almost three years ago, she was living with her seven preschool-aged grandchildren in a tiny mud-and-stick home, no larger than the average western toilet. The floor was cracked and broken, and each night the children would huddle together around *Gogo*, hoping to avoid the resident mice that nightly descended upon the home.

Matron and our team worked closely with *Gogo* and her community for several years. Together we grew a large-scale vegetable garden replete with everything from cassava to banana trees, enough to sustain her family. We also built her a beautiful new two-bedroom home complete with a separate toilet and water tank, the simplest of items that, for *Gogo*, had long seemed unattainable.

Recently, the Makhewu community gathered to celebrate the opening of *Gogo*'s new home. Even in her seventies, *Gogo* Ndzimandze was still immediately recognisable by her tall, statuesque frame and powerful features. The choir arrived before dawn and started cooking for the crowds who would gather. Chicken and rice was brought to the boil in large black pots over a central fire inside the cooking hut.

As the village roosters crowed in strangely jubilant harmony, heralding the first tendrils of morning light, *Gogo*'s homestead bustled with preparations for her special day.

Every inch of her home was meticulously swept with brooms made of tightly bound bundles of straw, the children were washed and dressed in their finest clothes, twenty plastic seats and several wooden benches that had been borrowed were arranged lovingly outside the home, and traditional drinks of fermented maize meal, *emaHewu*, were prepared in large blue tubs. As the activity swelled, the new home watched silently on.

Over the next several hours, a steady stream of people climbed the red dust roads to *Gogo*'s homestead.

A single drummer stood in the corner of the homestead with a handmade bongo drum. As he played, the choir rose to their feet and began singing and dancing. The music soon reached fever pitch as more and more people trickled into the little rural homestead.

When it was time for the ceremonies to begin, various community members took turns to sing and dance. Smiling children formed a ragged conga line and weaved through the throngs of people. Then, just as the little ones sat down, the *gogos* stood up and quickly took their place in the centre of the crowd. They swayed, waving their arms above their heads, and danced to a slow siSwati melody, laughing like school girls. As the community elders spoke, one by one, others stood and danced together to the beat of the drum—mothers with babies on their backs, priests dressed in bright red and green.

I sat with Matron in the shade and watched delightedly as the joyous scene unfolded before me. When the *Indvuna* finished speaking, it was my turn to address the community. As I rose from my plastic chair, I felt a hand on my shoulder. It was Matron.

'My son, before you speak, you must dance.'

Matron Anna Zwane and I rose quietly to our feet and motioned for *Gogo* Ndzimandze to join us. Together we danced and laughed, as the wild orange sun rose into the sky.

From Siteki with love,

Maithri

Being seen

The most common greeting heard in Swaziland is *'Sawubona'*. It means, 'I see you'.

There are many ways of seeing.

I remember, during my student years, reading Foucault's work on medical anthropology, particularly how he described 'the medical gaze'.

He postulated that when a health care worker meets a patient, the patient often becomes objectified, and is therefore dehumanised. Power, in most situations, resides with the health care worker and rarely with the patient.

I wish that were not the case, but I know that in many parts of the world it seems to be true. The situation arises not because health care workers are cruel—quite the contrary—but because of the nature of the work.

I believe that the vast majority of health care workers are genuinely compassionate individuals with a commitment to the welfare of those they serve. With so much to be done—so many patients to see; so little time for sleep, food, or self-care; and so many agendas and schedules to work through—it is little wonder that the medical gaze can become one that attempts to be as time efficient and detached as possible.

But there is far more to healing than just mechanically fixing a broken part. It is tantalisingly easy to take a 'fast food' approach to medicine in developing countries, trying to see as many patients as quickly as possible. And nowhere is that more apparent than in Africa.

Each morning we have patients travelling many kilometres, often on foot, to reach the hospital. They line up and often wait for hours in order to receive medical attention. As health care workers, it is our duty to provide care to every patient in a timely, efficient, and organised manner.

The need for more acute services, such as outpatient departments and clinics that are able to see hundreds and hundreds of sick people each day, is undeniable and deeply salient in the context of pandemics like AIDS and other endemic diseases.

However, we are also fully aware that so much of what we see in the hospital is a symptom or complication of pathological living circumstances, such as extreme poverty, abuse, and geographical or social isolation.

Often a child with dehydration secondary to chronic diarrhoea remains sick because of dirty drinking water. A man who has chronic skin infections despite multiple courses of antibiotics is often living in conditions of abject poverty and unhygienic surrounds.

Home-based care, which utilises a skilled team that is able to visit families directly within their communities and homesteads, is an effective adjunct to acute medical services, and it offers a distinct way of addressing many issues that we take for granted in other countries. The team at the Good Shepherd Hospital for example has a thirty-four-day cycle during which they visit thirty-four distinct, large rural communities, providing immediate, compassionate medical care.

In the context of medicine in rural Africa, I am a proponent of home-based care for the simple fact that it helps us to see the situation more clearly. It broadens our vision to include the origins of illness and the human and socioeconomic variables that perpetuate it.

When a health care worker enters a hut to visit a family or a patient, they are given an immediate and stark reminder of the cycle of disease and poverty, which is manifest throughout so much of sub-Saharan Africa.

Importantly, many of the patients seen by a home-based-care team at the Good Shepherd Hospital have stage four, terminal, AIDS and are suffering deeply. Often what those patients need more than anything else is not simply for us to see their illness, but to see their humanity; to hear and acknowledge the person that lies beneath the suffering.

For so many, when curative measures have failed, there is comfort in knowing that their personal struggle in the face of enormous adversity is validated—in receiving the simple acknowledgement that they have not been forgotten.

One of the great common denominators I have discovered from my experiences in Swaziland has been that when you have nothing—when you are dying a painful and solitary death—the smallest kindness, the most seemingly insignificant touch, the most cursory glance, means everything.

Health care in Africa and around the world is at its best when it addresses a basic primordial human need; the need for someone to look you in your eyes and say simply, from the heart, 'My brother, my sister, *sawubona*. I see you.'

From Siteki with love,

Maithri

siSwati pronunciation

a	'ah', as in 'Serbia'
e	'e', as in 'bet'
i	'i' as in 'spin' (at the beginning or middle of a word)
	'ee', as in 'bee' (at the end of a word)
o	'o', as in 'post'
u	'oo', as in 'tool'

dl	a soft breathy sound, close to 'gl' in 'glamour'
hl	produced with a harsh and forceful breath
k	'g', as in 'game'
kh	'k', as in 'take'
ng	as in 'sing'
t	'd', as in 'deep'
th	't', as in 'paste'

GLOSSARY

(siSwati – English)

babe	father
dokotela	doctor
gogo	grandmother
hamba embile	go straight
indvuna	leader below the Chief and leader of the *Umphakatsi*
kubuhlungu kuphi	where is the pain?
make	mother
Ngwenyama	title of the male ruler or king of Swaziland
sanibonani ekhaya	(literally 'hello house') is anyone home?
sawubona / sanibonani	(literally 'I see you') hello / hello to more than one person
siyabonga	thank you
umlungu	white person
umphakatsi	Community Committee
vula bevalile	open the closed door
yini inkinga	what is the problem?

Acknowledgements

I would like to express my gratitude to the many people who have been a part of my journey.

In Swaziland

The *Ngwenyama* of Swaziland for allowing us to work within the Kingdom.

The Minister of Health, the Regional Administrator of Lubombo, and Matron Simelane, who oversee health care within the Lubombo region. And Mr Eric Maziya, Regional Secretary of the Lubombo region, for his compassionate belief in our work.

The administrator of the Good Shepherd Hospital, Mrs Dumsile Simelane, and Senior Medical Officer, Dr Haile Petros, for their kind assistance.

All the doctors, nurses, and non-clinical staff at the Good Shepherd for their inspiration, camaraderie, and support over many years.

The entire team at Possible Dreams International—our local and international teams, volunteers, choir, ambassadors, and field partners. I am humbled by the extraordinary work that they undertake every day of the year. It is my great honour to be a part of the team and I am grateful to each of them for their compassionate service.

My hero, Matron Anna Zwane, for her wisdom and friendship.

The gracious people of Swaziland who continue to reveal to me the true meaning of courage and grace.

In Australia

The team at Ilura Press, in particular Christopher, Rafah, Elsie, and Sabina, for the extraordinary love, sensitivity, and respect they have shown these stories during the editing and publishing process. Thanks for helping this barefoot doctor feel like an author!

Debbi Long for her wonderful advice and lessons about ethnography and medical anthropology, which have forever changed the way I view medical and development work.

To my family—Ammi, Thathi, and Hithaishi—as the earth thanks the sun.

Maithri Goonetilleke is a medical doctor and executive director of Possible Dreams International. He came to Australia from Sri Lanka with his parents at an early age. He studied medicine at the University of Melbourne and has worked throughout Australia as both a general medical and emergency registrar—running sole-doctor emergency departments in rural areas, and working in Indigenous communities and in correctional institutions.

In Swaziland, through his work with Possible Dreams International, he provides emergency medical relief to those living with HIV/AIDS, malnutrition, and extreme poverty, as well as providing sustainable development solutions such as access to clean water, agriculture, income generation, and housing. When not in Swaziland or working in rural Australia, he resides in Melbourne.

vula bevalile

[voo-lah be-vah-li-le]